Insight Inspirations

Messages of Hope

by

Jane Tucker

Acknowledgement

With deepest gratitude to the late Sydney Banks, for sharing with humanity his profound insight into the three universal principles of Mind, Consciousness and Thought.

Meeting Syd over 37 years ago, and hearing the tiniest glimmer of what he was saying, changed my life forever. It awoke in me an awareness of the beauty, love, and wisdom that lie at the core of every single human being. It provided me with a foundation so strong, so stable, and so powerful that my life from that point on has been more beautiful than I ever could have imagined. The inevitable ups and downs have only served to deepen my understanding and strengthen my faith in the Truth of these principles.

Even though Mr. Banks is no longer with us in physical form, his materials offer everyone a chance to *hear* his enlightened message, directly from the source. In some unexplainable way, his books, the words and video on his archived website www.sydneybanks.org and his recorded talks have an unequalled power to deeply touch people's souls, awakening something within that they hadn't realized was there--true wisdom and unconditional love.

Introduction

Syd Banks said many times, "Only talk what you know." This little booklet contains insights that came to me as a result of listening to Syd and "looking within" for the answers we all seek.

The first few essays were written to give away at a street fair in a public housing community. People found them helpful, and began making copies to share with neighbors and friends. I was encouraged to put them into book form, and *Insight Inspirations: Messages of Hope* was self-published in 2000.

Since that time, educators, therapists and counselors have shared these messages with those they serve, and have expressed interest in having the booklets more readily available. For this reason, the current version is now in print

It is my sincere wish that these "Messages of Hope" will help anyone seeking peace of mind to recognize where it is found, and to experience it more and more deeply.

Insight Inspirations

Table Of Contents

The Gift

Deep down inside, all people are the same. We all share a precious gift, no matter who we are, where we come from, or whatever we've been through in life. Every one of us is born with a core of wisdom, common sense, compassion, and power. This is our birthright.

We all experience challenges in life, difficulties that may seem impossible to overcome. The good news is that within each of us is a source of comfort and true guidance. It is a Spiritual Connection that can never be broken. Sometimes, we can feel far away from this connection, caught up in the worries and problems of everyday life. The key to finding it again is very simple. All we have to do is remember that it's there.

It is only our own thinking that keeps us from seeing this. As human beings, we all have countless thoughts passing through our minds all the time. When we latch on to thoughts that bring us pain, we feel that pain, and we see the world through that lens. From this state of mind, we feel lost and far away from the peace that is our true nature.

What a relief it is to realize that thoughts are not permanent. They only last for as long as we give them life. Only our true self, our inner wisdom, our Spiritual Connection, is permanent and real. Knowing this eases the grip of negative thoughts. When we allow a painful thought to pass, without judging ourselves for having it, the beautiful feeling of who we really are brings us back into harmony with life.

Beyond Blame

When things go wrong, it's easy to find someone to blame. It might be society, or those in authority, but most often it turns out to be the ones closest to us -- the people we live with every day. Once we understand that our feelings are not really created by outside forces, but by our own thoughts, we are freed from the need to blame.

Blaming someone else for how we feel doesn't help us feel any better; it only justifies our hurt or anger. Blaming ourselves doesn't help either. Any time we harbor thoughts of blame, we keep the bad feelings going. From an angry, hurt or fearful feeling, it is impossible to find true solutions. When we allow the negative thoughts to pass, our minds quiet, and insights appear.

Wisdom comes via a beautiful feeling. If you feel good, enjoy it! It's your right and privilege to experience joy and happiness. The more we live in good feelings, the more quickly we notice when our thoughts are taking us in the other direction. As soon as we realize what is truly happening, we begin to regain our balance.

Courage

You might not think it takes courage to be happy, but sometimes it does. When our minds are full of negative thoughts, these thoughts can make us feel like we'll lose something if we stop thinking about them. We can get caught in a whirlpool of insecure thinking, swirling around and pulling us down deeper and deeper. All this fear and negativity can fall away in a second, though, if we have the courage to see it for what it is -- only thoughts. Nothing real, nothing true -- only an interpretation of life -- a dream we are choosing to believe.

The moment we accept our own part in creating the dream, it loses its power. That one moment puts things in perspective, and we see that we have a choice every second of our lives. If the choice is ours, why not create beauty? When we experience a beautiful feeling, it spreads out like ripples in a pond, touching everyone we meet.

Courage of this kind is rewarded immediately, and is accompanied by deep gratitude.

Finding Beauty

Every one of us is a beautiful, wise and loving human being. This is our core; it is who we are at heart. It is only mistaken thinking that causes us to see ourselves any other way. When we hold on to negativity, we cloud our vision. Instead of seeing a world full of beauty and promise, we see only the haze of our fearful, worried, or angry thinking.

We may believe we aren't as good as others, or that we can't succeed. These beliefs lose their power once we see they are only thoughts. Any negative idea that comes into our minds will fall away if we stop feeding it.

We "feed" these negative thoughts by dwelling on them, by giving ourselves examples from the past of why they are true. We also "feed" such thoughts when we try to fight them. The way to "disarm" such thinking is to remember that we are the ones thinking the thoughts. If I don't like the way I'm feeling, right now, it's because, right now, I'm thinking a thought that is creating that feeling. When the thought is allowed to pass, the feeling changes.

There's no reason why any one of us can't live a happy life. It's what we are made for. When we feel good within ourselves, we spread the feeling without even trying, and the world becomes a more beautiful place.

Quieting Down

In a quiet state of mind, we meet life's challenges with dignity, grace, and a sense of humor. In a quiet state of mind, we are open to wisdom. When we allow our thoughts to quiet down, letting go of "me," "my," "mine" and "I," a larger presence takes over, a presence of total comfort, ease, confidence, and unconditional love. This presence is available to every one of us, at any time. It is our "home," our birthright, a divine gift that is denied to no one.

We are the only ones who deny ourselves this gift, when we innocently focus on thoughts of lack, worry, fear, anger... when we forget the answer to life's challenges lies within ourselves, and not outside. Each one of us has access to wisdom that will guide us without fail. We only need to quiet down the chitter-chatter of our thoughts, and listen.

Having a quiet mind doesn't mean you
sit around doing nothing -- it's just the opposite.
When our minds are full of "busy-ness," and anx-
ious thoughts, we may run around a lot, but things
don't get done, or if they do, they never seem to be
done right.

On the other hand, when our minds are
calmer, we concentrate on whatever is in front of
us. We are in the present moment, and we give
our full attention to the needs of that moment. If a
child comes to us when we are in this clear state of
mind, we are present with the child, and more able
to respond with wisdom and love. If we are at work
and a problem comes up, we can see the solution
more easily. This is common sense. Life flows
when our thoughts are positive. A quiet mind is a
positive mind. When we feel negative, it just means
the mind has gotten cluttered up with insecure
(negative) thoughts.

Being Grateful

We all lose our way sometimes. I don't know anyone who hasn't, at one point or another, felt completely irritated or frustrated at someone else -- it could be a spouse, a child, a family member, or perhaps a co-worker or a neighbor.

Even though we may know deep down that it is our own thoughts creating the feeling, sometimes it is just too tempting to give in to blame, anger, judging, and in general being "ticked off." What can help at times like these is to remember a simple word: gratitude. The thought of gratitude -- gratefulness -- is extremely powerful.

When we remember to be grateful, all those
negative emotions die off. When we fill up with
gratefulness, there's no room for anything else.
A grateful feeling allows forgiveness to happen,
effortlessly. True gratitude feels so good, we don't
want to ruin it by bringing back all those ugly
feelings of blame and anger.

From a grateful feeling, we may be able to
reach the person who was "making us mad" and
truly communicate instead of just fighting; or, we
may see the wisdom of leaving that person alone
for a while. Whatever needs to be done about the
situation, gratitude will help us find the wisdom
to deal with it in the best way possible. A grateful
heart brings knowledge.

The Power
of Forgiveness

One of the most beautiful gifts we can give ourselves is to learn the art of forgiveness -- to see that when we hold resentment against anyone, we really hurt ourselves. Forgiveness brings freedom, and lets us live life more fully.

As long as we let thoughts about what someone else did or said churn around in our minds, we feel upset. The same thing happens when we hold unforgiving thoughts against ourselves. In this state of mind we don't see clearly, feel happy, or do our best. On the other hand, when we let go of a grudge, a lightness of spirit takes its place. In this more peaceful state of mind we find understanding, and joy.

Sometimes people see forgiveness as a sign of weakness. We may think that by forgiving someone who has hurt us, we're letting that person have some kind of control over us. Actually, the opposite is true. When we are unforgiving, we are the ones who suffer. Unforgiving thoughts hold us prisoner, keeping us in a state of stress and preventing us from feeling comfortable. Forgiveness is powerful. It frees us from the chains of a painful past.

To forgive does not mean to approve; we can forgive someone without approving of the behavior. It all comes down to the feeling we have inside. If someone is dangerous, it's common sense to stay away from that person, but it's possible to do this without carrying hate in our hearts. What forgiveness means is seeing that, deep down, we are all the same. We all make mistakes; we all have a lot to learn. Anyone can change.

Appreciation

Appreciation for the simple things of life --
how rich we are when we find this feeling! Again,
it's all a matter of remembering, being aware, being
grateful. Everyday chores can be meditations, family
members can be sources of joy, hard work can
be satisfying and fulfilling, difficult tasks can be
exciting challenges. Life is transformed when we
live in the present moment.

What stops us from living this way more of
the time? We may think it's stress -- pressures from
outside of ourselves -- but it really comes down to
what's going on in our own minds at any moment.

For example, we all know "money can't buy
happiness," but how often do we let concerns about
money fill our thoughts? We all know "worrying
doesn't solve anything," so why do we still do it?

Innocently, we let ourselves be fooled by our own misguided thoughts, instead of listening to the true guidance we have within, at a deeper level.

A valuable tool is to see our feelings as guide-posts. If we're feeling negative (sad, mad, fearful, etc.) it is a sign we're taking negative thoughts too seriously. If we can step back and even laugh (gently) at ourselves, we're way ahead of the game. Our natural good feelings will come back as soon as we let go of our hold on those unhappy thoughts. When we get back into the flow of life, appreciating our blessings and seeing the beauty around us and within us, our circumstances improve. It's a spiritual law ~ our inner wisdom will guide us in the right path, every time we let go of the thoughts that cover it up.

Strength

Being strong doesn't mean putting others down. Being truly strong means knowing that "who you are" is solid -- that we are all part of something far greater than any individual little self. The deeper we know this, the more we feel connected with this inner power, and the stronger we are. This kind of strength is not a threat to anyone. If someone sees it that way, it's only because his or her thinking is confused. This is a strength that is founded in love -- unconditional love that starts within yourself and extends outward.

This strength is protection. If I try to take care of myself with my ego, relying on my often mixed-up beliefs about the world, I'm in big trouble. If, instead, I realize that I have within a core of wisdom and universal intelligence, I can rely on that.

It's easy to tell the difference. When we rely on this inner Source, our actions feel right, and produce positive results. When we ignore this inner guidance, we often wind up feeling discontented, doubtful of our decisions, and in predicaments.

This is not to say life will be without challenges if we're on the right track. Everyone experiences ups and downs; that's part of being human. If we keep going back to our inner guidance, though, we will go through these trials with more understanding, and deepen our spiritual connection. This is the gift, the rainbow that appears, sometimes even in the midst of a storm.

Food for the Soul

There are times in life when we feel peace and harmony – when our thoughts are tranquil, and we are struck by the absolute beauty around us. These moments of clarity are precious. They let us see life anew.

How important it is to be open to such moments! So often, we feel we need to fill every minute with activity, and keep our minds "busy-busy," even during times of rest. What we really need is to find the time for quiet, peaceful reflection. It doesn't have to be a long time. Sometimes just sitting for a little while on the back porch, listening to the birds and appreciating the breezes, can bring a sense of gratitude and "all is well."

Walking in a park, watching children play, even resting on the living room sofa can be an opportunity to release the busy thoughts of the day and let peaceful feelings come. It's just a matter of stepping back for a moment from the hustle and bustle of the world.

Each time we experience these beautiful feelings, we become richer. As we open up to them more and more, we find ourselves becoming more patient, tolerant and loving toward ourselves and others. As we come to realize that these peaceful feelings are always available to us, we learn to find them even in busy times. We start to notice when our thinking is "carrying us away" and catch our breath, dipping into that deep pool of calm that has become so familiar. It's like re-energizing. There's nothing we need to do to find this peaceful center, except to remember that it's there.

Listening

There are teachers all around us, and
wisdom to be found, if we only listen. Listening
requires stillness of the mind. Something new can
only enter our minds when there is space -- when
our thoughts slow down enough to let an insight
come through. If we are always trying to "get
our point across," we can't hear anything except
our own voice. If, on the other hand, we have the
courage to put aside what we think, and realize we
might learn something from someone else's point of
view, we gain and grow.

Even a small child can be a source of
wisdom. In their innocence, children often see
things more clearly than adults. If we listen with an
open heart, we can learn from anyone.

Just because a person appears to be in worse circumstances than we are doesn't mean he or she can't teach us something. You never know who might offer a precious insight about life, but unless you're listening, you'll miss it.

We don't need to worry about losing anything by quieting down and listening. When we truly listen, we deepen our own wisdom ~~ connection. Then, when we speak from this inner wisdom, our words are powerful. It seems like an opposite, but when we truly listen, our speech becomes inspired. An inspired speaker will affect others far more than someone who is trying hard to convince people that he or she is "right."

When we listen to life, we recognize what is true. We recognize the truth from inside ourselves ~~ with a feeling of "Ah, yes." It may be something we haven't thought of before, but when we hear it, it's as if we always knew it.

Sharing

When we start to gain an understanding of how life works, it's natural to want to share it. We need to be careful, though. Telling people what they're doing "wrong" is the surest way to put them off, especially when they haven't asked for any advice! When we focus on others' mistakes, we are guaranteed to miss our own.

Just live what you know, yourself. If you see someone acting in a confused way, remember the innocence of the person, and remember that we can help others most by sharing a beautiful, loving feeling -- not by giving criticism.

Of course, if someone comes to us for help, we want to offer any insight we might have. The key is to do this with humility, remembering that it could easily be the other way around.

Grace

We all have moments when everything seems to "click." At these times, things happen effortlessly, and it feels as if we are being carried along through life, above the trials and annoyances that might otherwise disturb us. It is a wonderful feeling, and usually brings a smile and a thought of "Thank You." We may think of it as being in a "state of grace."

In truth, this gift of grace is always with us, always available to us. It comes when we are in tune with our own wisdom; when we are not trying to control anything in life, but rather allowing the beautiful rhythms of life to unfold around us. We only "fall out" of this state when our own thinking distracts us from it.

Hard Times

Everyone comes up against hard times in life ~ times when things happen that just seem like too much to bear. At such times, we may become overwhelmed by sadness or anger, and find ourselves drowning in an ocean of negative thoughts.

What can help is to remember that these feelings will not last forever. Be grateful for any rest from the rush of negative thoughts. This is where healing and comfort will arise.

Within each of us is a Source of love, patience, and kindness. When we turn to this Source, we find peace that lifts us above our sorrow. In the end, we will come through the hard times, better able to help others because of what we have experienced. We will have grown in wisdom and found a deeper understanding of life.

Humor & Friendship

A sense of humor is absolutely essential in life. Without it, we would be doomed to permanent misery! Much of our unhappiness comes from taking ourselves too seriously ~ thinking about ourselves so much that we lose all perspective. What a relief it is when we notice what we're doing, and see the humor in it. When this happens, we are lifted into a lighter, more accepting state of mind.

Light-heartedness is one of the best gifts we can bring to another person. If we let ourselves become filled with sadness when a friend is suffering, we don't really help that friend. If we take a friend's sorrow, fear or anger seriously, we are just adding fuel to the fire. Instead of helping her or him rise above the confusion, we create more of it.

True friendship is seeing beyond the suffering, to the perfect human being innocently caught up in negative thoughts. It is staying calm and centered, keeping a perspective, keeping a sense of humor. It is looking at your friend without judgment, realizing that we're all the same, and that no one is any better than anyone else.

Creativity

Creativity exists in abundance within each of us. It's not something we possess; it's an energy that is everywhere, and that will come through us as soon as we get out of the way. When we are thinking hard about life, we block this energy. Our worries, our concerns, our search for answers keep our minds busy, and we miss the insights that could come, if only we would slow down. There is no limit to what this creative energy can accomplish. It can make obstacles disappear, it can show us possibilities in unlikely places, it can provide solutions to "unsolvable" problems. It can help us to see people in a fresh way, so that instead of repeating old habits, we find newness in our relationships.

When we are open to creativity, we are open to change, knowing that we have nothing to fear. We participate more fully in life, enjoying the adventure of it. Instead of trying to figure out what we should do, we surprise ourselves with new ideas. We become part of the process of creation. It is the most natural thing in the world.

Aloha

In the islands of Hawai'i, the word "Aloha" is used to express many things. The deepest meaning of the word is spiritual. It refers to the breath ("ha") of God, the Divine Spirit that animates all creation. When someone speaks the word Aloha in its true sense, it is an acknowledgement of this Spirit in everyone and everything.

Aloha means Love, in all its forms; Love for a sweetheart, a child, a grandparent, a friend, a generation; Love for the ocean, the mountains, the stars in the heavens, for all of Life.

To live in Aloha is to live in harmony, to be humble, to be at peace.

Aloha means sharing. Whatever we have is a gift, and it is our privilege to share it. When we share our Aloha, we give what is best of ourselves, and we are blessed.

In the spirit of Aloha, nothing is impossible.

Security

As we learn to live in a quieter state of mind, we find ourselves becoming surer, more confident, and more at ease around all different kinds of people. This happens because when our minds are quiet, we are more open to our inner wisdom. We see beyond differences and feel empathy with others.

As we recognize that embarrassment or insecurity are only products of thought, we experience these feelings less and less. When they do occur, we can laugh them off, instead of taking them so seriously. This allows us to stay centered and "in the present." Such an attitude inspires calm in others, making communication easy and rewarding.

A loving heart, unencumbered by insecure thoughts, can move mountains. Eyes that look past appearances see beauty and innocence in every face. When we change on the inside, the world around us reflects this change. We see and experience a more positive and loving environment.

This "inside change" cannot be forced; we cannot make ourselves or anyone else change. It happens when we are truly ready; when we get a glimpse of a deeper reality and see its beauty. Then, we start to experience life differently. There is no end to the process. Gratitude and Patience are the keys.

Faith and Love

We really do not have to worry about the future. If we live according to our inner truth, we will be guided every step of the way. If our hearts' desire is to live in Love, we will not go wrong. Life will teach us the lessons we need to grow, and we will come through these lessons stronger and wiser.

Faith means knowing there is something greater than what we can figure out, and that this "Something Greater" has us, takes care of us, is us. It is the One Mind in which we all exist. Thoughts of lack, limitation or separateness are only illusion. Each time we experience this feeling, we grow into our own -- we find our way home.

The more we live in this feeling, the more understanding we have, and the less likely we are to do harm. Loving thoughts inspire us to share with others, and to give from the heart. In Love, we see beyond ourselves; we see our relationship with all of creation. Love allows Faith to flower.

Trusting Your Own Wisdom

Always go by your own inner feeling. Sometimes, we may think someone else is smarter than we are, and look to that person for answers to life's problems. No matter how smart someone else is, he or she cannot give us wisdom. We can only find wisdom within ourselves.

We can listen to someone else's words, and if they touch a chord within us, we will be inspired. We will be helped because what was said "rings true." We recognize it. If something doesn't "ring true," we would be foolish to accept it.

When we learn something from within ourselves -- when we have an insight -- that knowledge is ours forever. This is very different from believing someone else's ideas. Beliefs change constantly. When we discover Truth from within, it never changes; it only grows richer as our understanding deepens. There is no greater teacher than the one inside each one of us.

Note of Appreciation

Heartfelt thanks to my dear husband for his deep love and constant support; to our grown-up children who never cease to amaze and inspire me; to our life-long friends who beautifully demonstrate love in action every day; and to all those carrying on the legacy of Sydney Banks, helping to awaken humanity to the profound realization of who and what we really are.

Printed in Great Britain
by Amazon.co.uk, Ltd.,
Marston Gate.